This book belongs to:

_____

_____

_____

CHAPTER 1

Starting out

Jesus cares about you. He loves you so much that He wants you to be God's friend and a member of God's family.

God created people to be His friends. But not all people listen to God. They choose to try to live without Him. The Bible calls this sin.

Holy God

No Sin

Sin

Do we sin?

Do we say or do bad things? Read **Romans 3:23** (this means Romans, chapter 3, verse 23) to see what God says about this.

> ***For all have sinned and fall short of the glory of God.***

God says in the Bible that trying to be good or trying to please Him is not enough to take away our sin.

Only God can take away our sin.
Read **Ephesians 2:8–9.**

> ***For it is by grace you have been saved, through faith— and this not from yourselves, it is the gift of God—not by works, so that no one can boast.***

We cannot do enough good things to get to God by ourselves.

Holy God

Sin

be good

go to church

No Sin

2

But, even though we sin, God still loves us. He loves us so much that He has made a way to take away our sin and not punish us for it. Jesus takes our punishment for us.

Which is the way to remove sin?

Blaming others   Being good   JESUS   Singing pretty

NO WAY!

SIN IS REMOVED

What do you know about Jesus? Draw a picture of one story you know about Him.

Jesus never did anything bad or sinful. Yet He was willing to die on the cross for us to take the punishment for our sin. Three days later, God the Father raised Jesus from the dead. He had power over sin and death.

When Jesus died for our sin and rose from the dead, He became the only way to bridge the gap between sinful people like us and God.

If we tell God we are sorry for our sin, God promises to forgive us and make us clean inside. Read **1 John 1:9.**

If we confess our sins, he is faithful and just and will forgive us our sins and purify us from all unrighteousness.

P	B	C	Q	B	H	Z	R	I	B
S	P	Z	T	Q	D	Q	I	Z	E
D	P	T	B	O	B	W	Z	A	Q
S	H	P	A	Q	W	Z	A	P	Y
O	Z	U	R	S	I	Q	N	P	B

Cross out Q, Z, P, and B to find the hidden message. Write the remaining letters here:

— — — — — — — — —

— — — — — — — — —

— — — — — — !

Answer: Christ died to wash away our sin!

When we trust Jesus to take away our sin, He takes it away forever.

When Jesus takes away your sin, God welcomes you into His family. He wants you to talk to Him, to learn about Him and to love Him. He wants you to keep trusting Jesus and turn away from the things He has asked you not to do.

Not only does God forgive your sin when you trust Jesus, but He gives His Holy Spirit to live in you and guide your life. One day you will live with God in heaven forever.

> *I give them eternal life, and they shall never perish; no one can snatch them out of my hand.* **John 10:28**

WRITE YOUR NAME IN THE BLANKS

For God so loved _____ that He gave His

one and only Son, that if _____ believes

in Him, _____ shall not perish but

_____ will have eternal life.

John 3:16

God's Holy Spirit in our lives helps us know what is right and what is wrong and helps us to do things that are right.

God cannot tell lies. He always keeps His promises. If your feelings make you doubt whether you are really a Christian, remember that God always keeps His promises. God says, "I will never leave you or forsake you."

REMEMBER ...

Jesus Christ is the same yesterday and today and forever.

Hebrews 13:8

CHAPTER 2

The Bible

You need the Bible to help you grow stronger as a Christian. Without the help of the Bible you would soon find it very difficult to follow Jesus.

MORE BIBLES HAVE BEEN PRINTED THAN ANY OTHER BOOK.

You will find the Bible exciting; it will become very precious to you. Thousands of years ago, God gave people the words He wanted them to write in the Bible. You will be really interested in what He has written for you.

God's library

The Bible is really a whole library of books put together. It is divided into two main parts. Fill in the blanks by looking in your Bible.

How many books make up the Old Testament? _____

How many books make up the New Testament? _____

The last book in the Old Testament is _____.

The book of Galatians is in the _____ Testament.

The first book in the Bible is _____.

Answers: 39, 27, Malachi, New, Genesis

Genesis

Psalms

Zechariah

Malachi

Mark

John

Acts

Romans

2 Corinthians

Galatians

11

Information

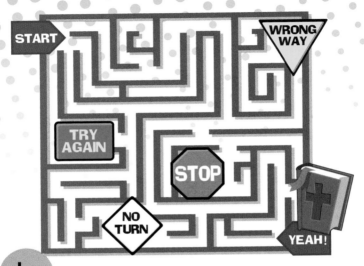

Life can be very confusing and difficult. It is easy to make mistakes and wrong choices. The Bible helps us get through the maze.

Some road signs give us important information. If we miss a sign or pay no attention to it, we may go the wrong way or have an accident.

The Bible has information about God and people, the past, the present, and the future. So we need to read it carefully.

12

Instructions

It does not matter whether we are building a house or repairing a bike, we must follow the instructions. Things will only fit together properly if we do.

God knows the very best way for us to live our lives. He has put a set of instructions in the Bible. See how many instructions you can find in **Exodus 20:1-17.** Read this in your Bible and write down some of the instructions God gave us: _____

_____

_____

Growing

To make sure we grow and become strong, we need to eat good food every day. If we stop eating, our bodies will become very weak. Read **1 Peter 2:2–3.**

Like newborn babies, crave pure spiritual milk, so that by it you may grow up in your salvation, now that you have tasted that the Lord is good.

The Bible is spiritual food for Christians. By reading what God has said in the Bible and doing what the Bible says, you will grow spiritually. So every day, read a few verses of the Bible.

Start by reading through the gospel of Luke in one month. You can follow the schedule on the next page.

Schedule

Schedule for reading the gospel of Luke in one month:

•**DAY 1:**	Luke 1:1–38	•**DAY 16:**	Luke 12:13–50
•**DAY 2:**	Luke 1:39–80	•**DAY 17:**	Luke 12:51–13:30
•**DAY 3:**	Luke 2:1–38	•**DAY 18:**	Luke 13:31–14:35
•**DAY 4:**	Luke 2:39–3:38	•**DAY 19:**	Luke 15
•**DAY 5:**	Luke 4:1–32	•**DAY 20:**	Luke 16
•**DAY 6:**	Luke 4:33–5:26	•**DAY 21:**	Luke 17
•**DAY 7:**	Luke 5:27–6:26	•**DAY 22:**	Luke 18
•**DAY 8:**	Luke 6:27–7:17	•**DAY 23:**	Luke 19:1–35
•**DAY 9:**	Luke 7:18–50	•**DAY 24:**	Luke 19:36–20:26
•**DAY 10:**	Luke 8:1–39	•**DAY 25:**	Luke 20:27–21:6
•**DAY 11:**	Luke 8:40–9:17	•**DAY 26:**	Luke 21:7–22:6
•**DAY 12:**	Luke 9:18–51	•**DAY 27:**	Luke 22:7–53
•**DAY 13:**	Luke 9:52–10:29	•**DAY 28:**	Luke 22:54–23:25
•**DAY 14:**	Luke 10:30–11:26	•**DAY 29:**	Luke 23:26–24:12
•**DAY 15:**	Luke 11:27–12:12	•**DAY 30:**	Luke 24:13–53

Competition

In the front of your Bible, you will find a list of all the books of the Bible. Use this list to do the following activities.

Matching: Draw lines to connect the books with the Testament they belong in.

MATTHEW

ISAIAH

REVELATION

GALATIANS

HOSEA

ROMANS

OBADIAH

PSALMS

JAMES

Answers: New Testament: Matthew, Revelation, Galatians, Romans, James
Old Testament: Isaiah, Hosea, Obadiah, Psalms

Unscramble the names of the following books of the Bible:

HOJNA

_ _ _ _ _

KLEU

_ _ _ _

OUXSDE

_ _ _ _ _ _

BJO

_ _ _

UHTR

_ _ _ _

ISTTU

_ _ _ _ _

ALOCONSSSI

_ _ _ _ _ _ _ _ _ _

Just for fun, see how many names of the books of the Bible you can learn by next week. Maybe in a month or so you will learn them all!

CHAPTER 3
Talking with God

Imagine what it would be like if you didn't talk to your family or friends for a whole week! How would you feel? How would they feel?

Now that you are part of God's family, He wants you to talk with Him. Talking with God is called praying.

God always hears

Sometimes people can be too busy to listen to you. But God is never too busy. He is never tired or asleep. He always listens when you pray.

God always answers

Some people think that if they do not get everything they ask for, God did not answer.

God is our loving Father. When we ask Him for something, He answers in one of three ways:

- Sometimes God says "**No.**" That's because He loves us and knows that what we have asked for is not the best for us.

- Sometimes God says "**Wait.**" We have to be patient and go on praying until we see His answer.

- Sometimes God says "**Yes.**" Right away we see the answer.

How should we pray?

We can pray out loud or just think the words in our minds. Sometimes we close our eyes to help us concentrate on God. Other times we pray with our eyes open.

Sometimes we kneel to pray or bow our heads. This shows that we want to give God our respect.

When we say "Amen" at the end of a prayer, it is to show that we agree with what has been said.

Where should we pray?

We can pray anywhere: at home, at church, and with our friends.

REMEMBER ...
God always hears.

When should we pray?

It is good to have a special time each day to pray. But God does not want you to pray to Him only at that time. He wants you to remember to talk with Him anytime.

Sometimes you will pray alone, and sometimes you will pray with other people. Read **Ephesians 6:18.**

And pray in the Spirit on all occasions with all kinds of prayers and requests. With this in mind, be alert and always keep on praying for all the saints.

Color the boxes that have dots to find a hidden message.

Answer: Pray all the time.

23

What should we pray?

LOVE HIM

When we pray, we should first tell God how much we love Him.

THANKS

We should be thankful to God. He has given us everything to enjoy. He loves us, for we are His children.

SORRY

When we have done wrong, we pray for God's forgiveness and ask Him to help us do what is right.

PLEASE

God wants us to pray for others, too.

They may live in our own hometown or in other places. Do not forget to pray for your friends and family.

God likes us to talk to Him about the things that are important to us. Nothing is too difficult for God to do, and nothing is too small for Him to bother with.

Read Philippians 4:6.

Do not be anxious about anything, but in everything, by prayer and petition, with thanksgiving, present your requests to God.

CHAPTER 4

Facing problems

All of our problems do not disappear when we become Christians.

Think about a problem you have already faced.

You never have to face difficulties alone.
The Holy Spirit has come to help you.

Problems for Christians come to us in three ways: ourselves, the world, and the devil.

26

Ourselves

Remember, when we become Christians, God gives us a brand-new life. Sometimes, we find that we still want to please ourselves rather than God. This is because there is a struggle going on between our old life and our new life.

Our new life needs to grow and become stronger.

Fill in the missing letter in each phrase to find several things that will help you become a strong Christian.

THA____K GOD
BIBL____ STUDY
____ORSHIP

SHOW____OVE
PRA____SE GOD
____ORGIVE
OB____Y GOD

When I became a Christian, God gave me a
_____ _____. *(Read down the "missing letters" to find the answer.)*

Answer: NEW LIFE

Check things that will help you grow as a Christian

❑ **1.** pleasing yourself first

❑ **2.** loving and obeying God

❑ **3.** forgetting the Bible

❑ **4.** talking with God in prayer

❑ **5.** only talking with friends who are not Christians

❑ **6.** meeting with other Christians

Answers: 2, 4, 6

Read *2 Corinthians 5:17.*

Therefore, if anyone is in Christ, he is a new creation; the old has gone, the new has come!

According to this verse, what happens when you become a Christian?

_____

_____

The world

Many people in the world do not live God's way. Some Christians find that their families or friends have little time for Jesus. Even our friends may wonder why our lives are changing.

As Christians we want to put Jesus first in our lives. Things like money, sports, or clothes are good, but if they become more important than Jesus, they will stop our life from growing.

Some friends may laugh at us for reading our Bibles or going to church. There may be some things they want you to do that you know are wrong. You might feel lonely if you do not go along with them.

Difficult things happened to the Lord Jesus, too, so He understands how we feel.

Read **Hebrews 13:5–6.**

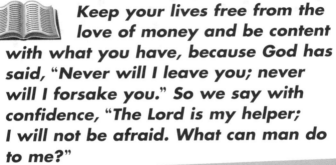

Keep your lives free from the love of money and be content with what you have, because God has said, "Never will I leave you; never will I forsake you." So we say with confidence, "The Lord is my helper; I will not be afraid. What can man do to me?"

Write down what God promises, and see if you can learn these verses by heart.

_____

_____

_____

_____

The devil

The devil is God's greatest enemy. He will always try to spoil our lives with sin. So, the devil will tempt us to do wrong things. He will try to make us doubt God's promises. He will make us think that we are not really in God's family. He will make us afraid to follow Jesus.

Jesus was tempted by the devil to do wrong. But He did not believe the devil's lies and answered by telling the devil verses from the Bible. Jesus defeated the devil by knowing and using God's Word.

IT IS WRITTEN!

The devil will lie to us. But we have the help of the Holy Spirit to answer him and to give us the strength not to give in.

The devil may say to us, "It does not matter if you steal." We can answer him, "Go away! God says it is wrong to steal. I won't do it." See what God says in *Exodus 20:15*.

Connect the dots to see where God's instructions are found.

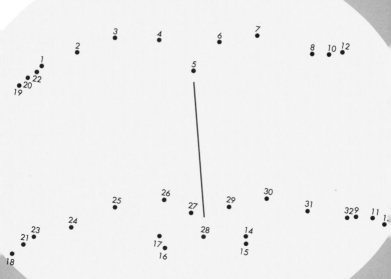

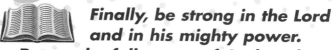

Read *Ephesians 6:10–11.*

Finally, be strong in the Lord and in his mighty power. Put on the full armor of God so that you can take your stand against the devil's schemes.

What do these verses tell us to do?

_____

_____

_____

_____

_____

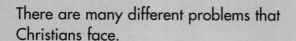

There are many different problems that Christians face.

God knows that sometimes you will sin and feel very sorry about it. You may think that God does not love you or want you in His family anymore.

What can you do? You can confess your sin to God and ask Him to forgive you.

Match the armor

Read *Ephesians 6:10–19* and match the object with the correct meaning.

1. Righteousness

2. Gospel of Peace

3. Truth

4. The Word of God

5. Salvation

6. Faith

Turn back to God's way

Ask God to strengthen you to live as a Christian. Remember, if you are trusting Jesus, God has forgiven your sin and brought you into His family—and no one can take you out of His family.

REMEMBER:

If I am trusting _____

God has forgiven all my _____.

He has brought _____ into

His _____. No one

can take me out.

CHAPTER 5

God's family

God's family is big!

In every part of the world, we find members of God's family. They may look different from us or speak a different language. But, if they trust Jesus, they are part of God's family.

Sometimes God's family is called "the Church" or "the body of Christ."

Although there is only one family, Christians meet in different places. Often these places are called churches.

Read **Acts 2:46–47.**

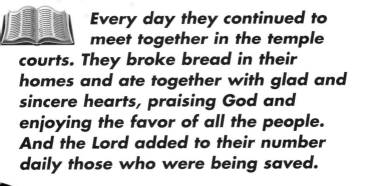

Every day they continued to meet together in the temple courts. They broke bread in their homes and ate together with glad and sincere hearts, praising God and enjoying the favor of all the people. And the Lord added to their number daily those who were being saved.

Write down some of the things that the first Christians did.

_____

_____

_____

_____

_____

Draw pictures of some of the things that happen in the church you go to.

Christians meet together to praise God and to remember what Jesus has done. Singing, praying, and learning from the Bible are fun.

Sometimes we do these things together. At other times, children, teenagers, and adults meet to do these things separately.

In church services, it is usually the adults who lead. But there are often parts when everyone joins in. Sometimes in services we laugh as we enjoy being together as the family of God. Other times, we are more serious and listen carefully to what is being said.

39

Christians enjoy meeting together. They encourage each other by talking and praying together.

When someone is sad or has a problem, the other family members are called to love and care for that person. Do you know someone you can help in this way?

Who: _____

_____

We also tell each other the good things that happen and the ways God helps us each day. Could you tell your friends something from your own life?

What: God loves you!

_____

_____

_____

_____

When we help each other, we start to feel that we really are members of God's family.

Every person in God's family is important. God tells us to encourage one another so that we all become strong Christians.

Read **Romans 12:4–5.**

Just as each of us has one body with many members, and these members do not all have the same function, so in Christ we who are many form one body, and each member belongs to all the others.

Talk about ways we can encourage each other in God's family.

We are so glad to be part of God's family that we want others to belong to God's family also.

We can invite our friends and family to church services or special events. Sometimes we go out together into the neighborhood to tell other people the Good News of Jesus.

Write down some things you could tell others about Jesus.

_____

_____

_____

_____

_____

_____

_____

_____

Even in God's family, we do not get along with everyone all the time. Sometimes there may be disagreements or we may feel upset or left out.

God says that we should talk about any problems and forgive one another just as He has forgiven us. Read **Hebrews 10:24–25.**

And let us consider how we may spur one another on toward love and good deeds. Let us not give up meeting together, as some are in the habit of doing, but let us encourage one another—and all the more as you see the Day approaching.

We need each other so that we can learn how to live as Christians.

CHAPTER 6

Telling others

Jesus wants all the people in God's family to act like Him. So our lives will gradually be changing. We will stop doing some things and start doing others. People should notice this difference and want to join God's family as well.

Write or draw the members of your family at home.

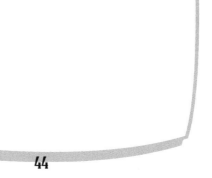

Whether there are lots of people living in your home or just a few, Jesus wants your life to show that you really love God.

Do you see ways to show love?

share your cookies

keep your room clean

hit your brother

hug your mom

send a birthday card

break a window

complain a lot

say "I love you"

How else could you show love?

_____

_____

At school

Our friends and teachers at school are all important to God. We should show that we belong to God's family there as well.

Describe a problem at school.

_____

_____

Read **Ephesians 4:31–32.**

Get rid of all bitterness, rage and anger, brawling and slander, along with every form of malice. Be kind and compassionate to one another, forgiving each other, just as in Christ God forgave you.

How does this verse help us with our problem?

_____

_____

_____

COLOR THE PICTURE ABOVE

47

Telling others

Jesus wants us to speak about Him to our families and friends.

You may have the chance to do this when others ask you why you do things differently.

LET ME TELL YOU ABOUT JESUS!

Read **Matthew 28:19–20.**

Therefore go and make disciples of all nations, baptizing them in the name of the Father and of the Son and of the Holy Spirit, and teaching them to obey everything I have commanded you. And surely I am with you always, to the very end of the age.

It is not always easy

Telling other people about Jesus can be hard. Some of your friends might not want to listen or they may laugh at you. Don't worry. In time they may see how different your life is and want to know why.

Other friends will be glad to listen right away.

Always remember Jesus' promise, **_I am with you always_** _(Matthew 28:20)._

Jesus' promise shows you He will never let you down.

There are three important things to remember when telling other people about Jesus.

1. Tell them stories about Jesus.

2. Tell them how you came to belong to God's family.

3. Do not force people to listen to you or be rude to them.

You can tell others about Jesus at home and school. Are there other places you can think of where you could do this as well?

_____

_____

_____

Even though you have come to the end of this *Discovery Book*, you will want to go on learning more about Jesus.

So,

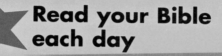

Read your Bible each day

Remember the schedule on page 15

Pray regularly

Meet with other Christians in your school or church

Ask older Christians for help—they will be very pleased you have asked them.

_____

_____

_____

Leader's Guide

This book was designed to be a personal study for a child to complete alone, with another individual as a partner or encourager, or for discussion in a small group. If used for small group study you will want to set aside one hour per week for six weeks to complete the lesson. A good sized group is 6–8 children.

The purpose of our study is to discover more about Jesus. You will need to read through each lesson ahead of time, completing the lesson yourself and preparing questions that you can ask to help the children understand the chapter. The small group time together is simply starting at the beginning of each chapter and discussing each topic so that you are certain that the children understand.

Chapter 1 can be done in class when you have the children together for the first time. Discuss each section of the chapter as you complete it. Chapters 2 and following can be completed each week prior to everyone's returning for the class time. In this way, you will have more time for discussion.

Make the time fun and friendly. Think of games you can use to get acquainted and to help understand the various points about Jesus.

Following are some helpful hints for you to use as leader.

1. Good leaders talk less than 20 percent of the time. Use questions to guide the discussion. Good questions ...
   • Cannot be answered "Yes" or "No."
   • Are stated simply.
   • Have several possible replies.

2. Let the children answer questions spontaneously rather than calling on certain individuals.

3. Never fear silence. If a pause seems too long, check to see if everyone understands and restate your question if necessary.

4. Stick to the subject. Don't allow the group to get sidetracked.

5. Don't allow one child to dominate. Encourage everyone to participate.

6. Encourage the children to apply the lesson to their own lives.

7. Always close the time together with prayer.

8. Thank you for investing in the lives of children by leading this study.

Notes:

Notes: